Sally

Lehrwerk für den
Englischunterricht ab Klasse 3

Activity Book 4

Erarbeitet von
Martina Bredenbröcker
Daniela Elsner
Stefanie Gleixner
Simone Gutwerk
Marion Lugauer

Unter Beratung von Jane Brockmann-Fairchild

Illustriert von
Monica May, Wilfried Poll,
Thilo Pustlauk und Gisela Vogel

Oldenbourg

Inhalt

Let's count!

1. Find the differences. What's missing in picture number 2?

2. Complete the lists. Work with a partner and compare.

Picture number 1:	Picture number 2:
There are ____ computers.	There is ____ computer.
There are ______________.	There are ______________.
There are ______________.	There are ______________.
There are ______________.	There are ______________.
There are ______________.	There are ______________.
There are ______________.	There are ______________.
There are ______________.	There are ______________.
There are ______________.	There are ______________.

chairs pencils pupils rulers tables pens schoolbags

Numbers

1. Cut out the puzzle (page 43), match the numbers and stick in.

two	four	nine	seven
six	eight	three	five
eleven	ten	twelve	one

2. Write down the numbers.

1 ____________ 2 ____________ 3 ____________

4 ____________ 5 ____________ 6 ____________

7 ____________ 8 ____________ 9 ____________

10 ____________ 11 ____________ 12 ____________

3. How much is it?

one + three = ____________ seven + five = ____________

two + six = ____________ eight + three = ____________

six + four = ____________ nine + one = ____________

What time is it?

1. Listen and number the clocks.

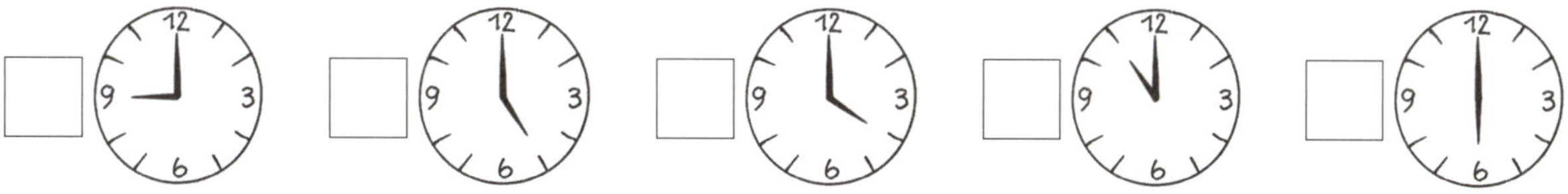

2. Listen and tick ✔ the correct time.

Lunchtime!

The time

1. Draw lines.

It's three o'clock. | It's twelve o'clock. | It's nine o'clock.

It's five o'clock. | It's eleven o'clock. | It's eight o'clock.

2. Set the clock. Draw the clock's hands.

It's one o'clock. | It's eleven o'clock. | It's four o'clock. | It's seven o'clock.

3. What time is it?

 It's ______________________.

 ______________________.

 ______________________.

 ______________________.

 ______________________.

 ______________________.

Kangaroo's action rhyme

Kangaroo, kangaroo,

______________________________ .

Kangaroo, kangaroo,

______________________________ .

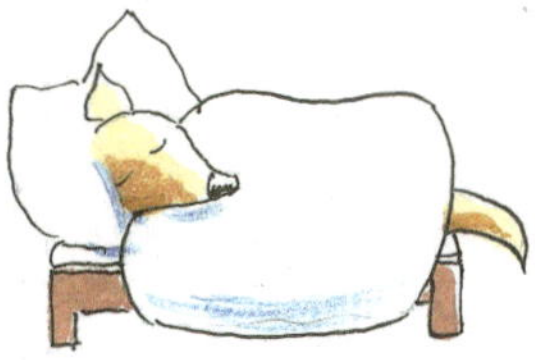

Kangaroo, kangaroo,

______________________________ .

Kangaroo, kangaroo,

______________________________ .

Kangaroo, kangaroo,

______________________________ .

Kangaroo, kangaroo,

______________________________ .

1. Number the pictures.

2. Write in the missing words.

Kangaroo, kangaroo, open the door.
Kangaroo, kangaroo, touch the floor.
Kangaroo, kangaroo, jump up the stairs.
Kangaroo, kangaroo, count the chairs.
Kangaroo, kangaroo, shake your head.
Kangaroo, kangaroo, go to bed.

Rooms

1. Write down the names of the rooms.

kitchen	bathroom	garden	bedroom	toilet	living room

2. Where are the children? Find the correct answer.

Yes, he is.	Yes, she is.	No, he isn't.	No, she isn't.

 Is Liz in the living room? ______

 Is Emily in the kitchen? ______

 Is Eric in the garden? ______

 Is Tim in the living room? ______

 Is Susan in the bathroom? ______

 Is Eric in the toilet? ______

 Is Phil in the garden? ______

 Is Emily in the bedroom? ______

Too big – too small

1. Is it just right? Read, choose your answer, write and draw.

Yes, it's just right.	No, it's too big.	No, it's too small.

Is the bath just right for Susan?

No, it's too small.

Is the sofa just right for Tim?

____

Is the bed just right for Phil?

____

Is the chair just right for Liz?

____

Is the door just right for Emily?

____

2. Listen and number in the correct order.

- ◯ just right
- ◯ living room
- ◯ kitchen
- ◯ garden
- ◯ bedroom
- ◯ bathroom

Furniture

1. Count the pieces of furniture and colour them. Work with a partner and compare.

There are ________ beds.

There are ________ tables.

There are ________ shelves.

There are ________ cupboards.

There are ________ desks.

There are ________ stereos.

There are ________ chairs.

There are ________ lamps.

There are ________ sofas.

2. Do the crossword.

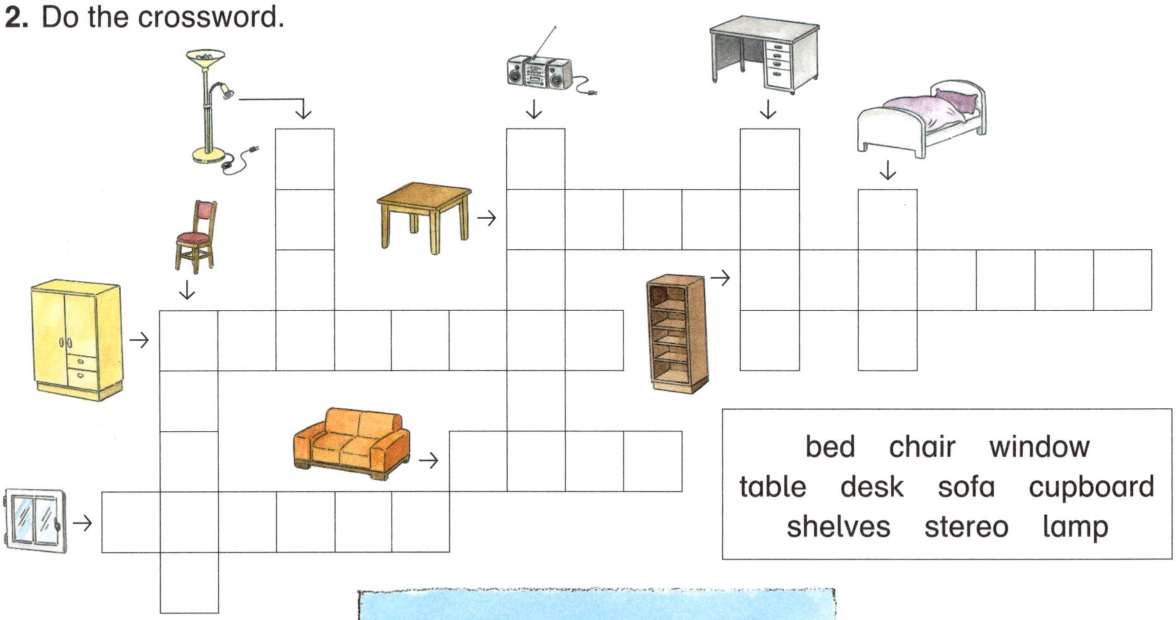

bed chair window
table desk sofa cupboard
shelves stereo lamp

My home is my castle!

Susan's room

1. Cut out the furniture (page 43). Listen and stick the furniture in.

2. Complete the sentences. Read your text to your group.

The bed is under the ______________________________.

The sofa is ______________________________.

The desk is ______________________________.

The cupboard is ______________________________.

The lamp is ______________________________.

The shelves are between the __________ and the __________.

in front of	next to	behind	under		
bed	small window	door	sofa	big window	desk

Let's make a sandwich!

1. Find the words and circle ◯ them.

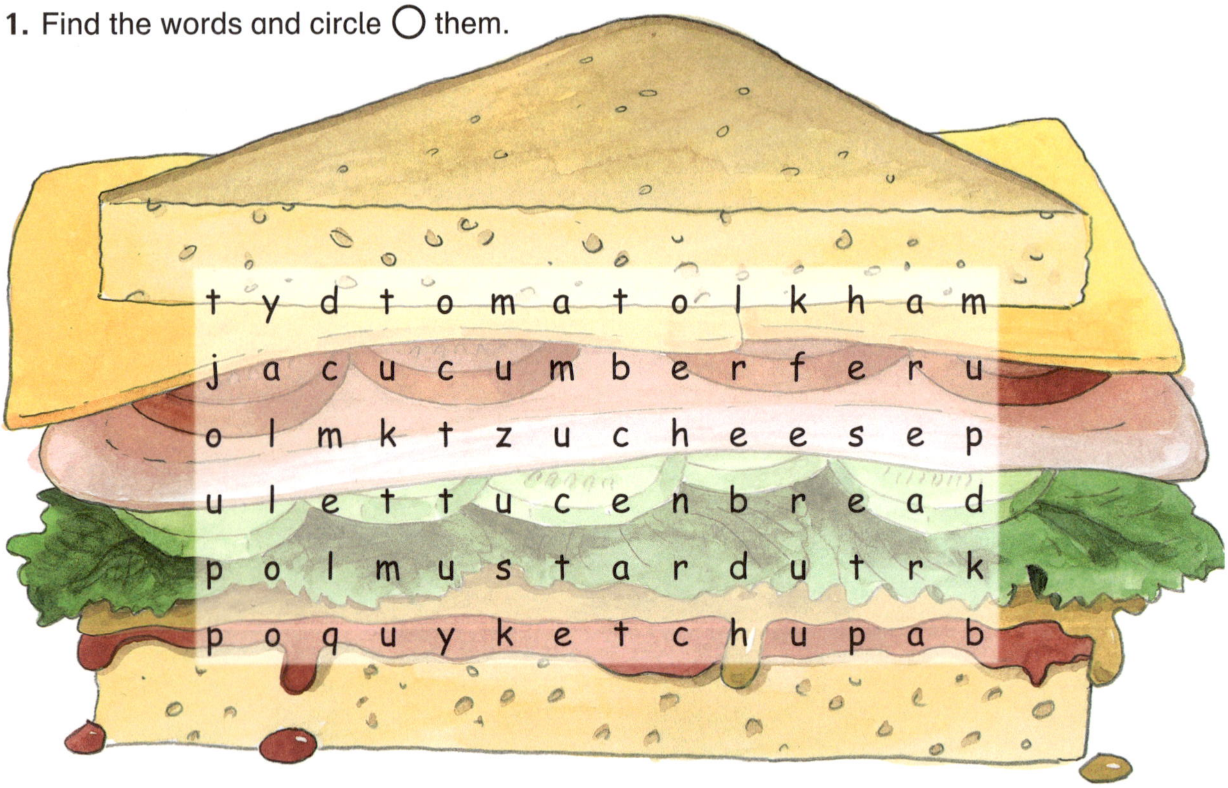

lettuce	ketchup	ham	cucumber	bread	cheese	tomato	mustard

2. Draw your own sandwich. Write down what you put in it.

______________ 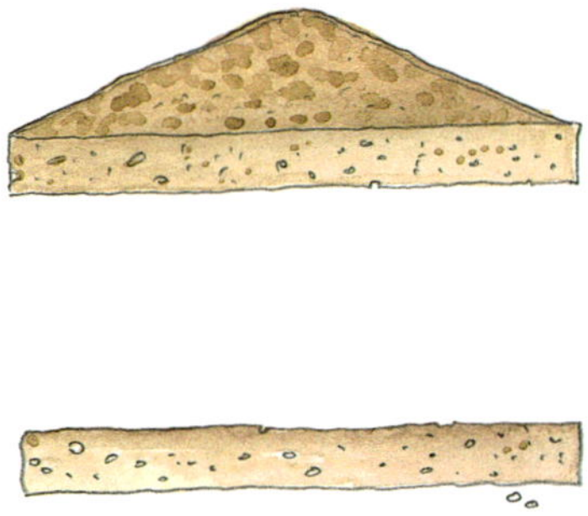 ______________

______________ ______________

______________ ______________

3. Listen to the song and tick ✔ the correct sandwich.

 ☐

 ☐

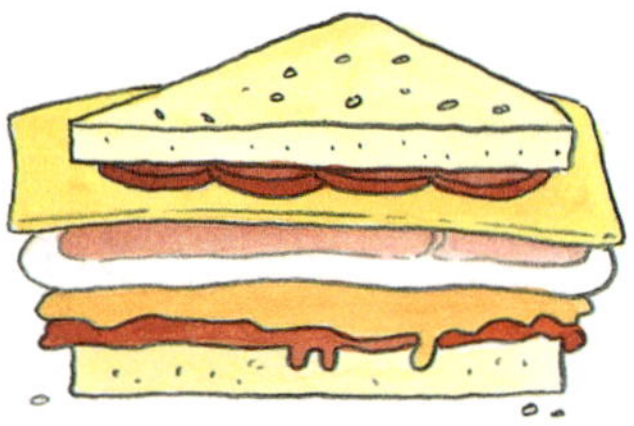 ☐

The sandwich is made out of: ______________________________

____

It's time for lunch!

1. Read the menu.

2. Write your own menu plan. Tell your partner.

Monday: ______________________

Tuesday: ______________________

Wednesday: ______________________

Thursday: ______________________

Friday: ______________________

3. In the dining hall: Listen and match.

Monday

Tuesday

Wednesday

Thursday

Friday

4. Listen again. What's missing? Draw.

Let's lay the table!

1. Lay the table for eight people. Count and draw.

2. What's missing? Complete the sentence and read it to your partner.

___ forks, ___ plates, ___ knives, ___ cup, ___ spoon,

___ glasses are missing.

3. Which answer is correct? Write it down.

You eat soup with it: It's a ______________ .

You need it for cutting: It's a ______________ .

You put lemonade in it: It's a ______________ .

You eat from it: It's a ______________ .

You pick up food with it: It's a ______________ .

You drink tea out of it: It's a ______________ .

In the restaurant

1. Listen and complete the speech bubbles.

2. Make up the dialogue. Write it down.

Frage, ob du helfen kannst.

Bestelle etwas zu essen.

Frage nach Getränken.

Bestelle etwas zu trinken.

Sage, wie viel es kostet.

Bezahle und verabschiede dich.

3. Say the tongue twister.

Sly Sam slurps Sally's soup.

Through the day

1. Listen to the song.

2. Cut out the text (page 45), match and stick it in.

3. Set the clock. Draw the clock's hands.

Hickory, dickory, dock!
The mouse ran up the clock.
The clock struck one.
The mouse ran down.
Hickory, dickory, dock!

One day in the life of Alpha 72

At 3 o'clock

I ______ .

At 4 o'clock

I have ________ .

At 5 o'clock

I ______ my hair.

At 6 o'clock

I ________ .

We ______ to fly.

At 10 o'clock

I have ______ .

At 1 o'clock

I ____________ .

At 2 o'clock

I ______ with my pet.

At 4 o'clock

I ______ my friends.

At 6 o'clock

I __________ .

learn	go to bed	get up	brush	go to school	breakfast
call	lunch	do my homework	play		

1. Listen.
2. Cut out the pictures (page 45), match and stick them in.
3. Write in the missing words.

My day

in the morning

in the afternoon

in the evening/at night

get up
learn at school have lunch
play (ball) with my friends
go to bed and sleep

1. What's your day like? Write and draw.

2. Tell your class about your day.

What's your hobby?

1. Draw lines.

swimming
riding a mountain bike
playing the guitar
reading books
ice skating
playing the piano
snowboarding
playing football
riding a horse

2. Complete the sentences.

Susan likes ______________________________.

Tim likes ______________________________

and ______________________________.

Emily likes ______________________________

and ______________________________.

Eric likes ______________________________.

Phil likes ______________________________

and ______________________________.

Liz likes ______________________________.

This is me!

1. Listen. Write in the missing words.

Hi, my ____________ is Will.

I'm ____________ years old.

I ____________ in Chester.

I'm in ____________ 4f.

My ____________ are football and

playing ________________________ .

Hello, my ____________ is Jenny.

I'm ____________ years old.

I ____________ in Chester, too.

I'm in ____________ 5d.

My hobbies are ____________ and

playing ____________________ .

name ten eleven class live computer games singing basketball hobbies

2. Draw a picture of yourself or stick in a photo.

3. Write about yourself.
Read your text to your class.

Hi, my name is ________________________

____

____

____

____

____

An interview with a sports star

Do your own interview, write it down and act it out.
Work with a partner.

Begrüße den Sportstar und frage, wie es ihm/ihr geht.

Sage, wie es dir geht.

Frage, ob er/sie Volleyball spielen kann.

Bejahe.

Frage, ob er/sie auch Klavier spielen kann.

Verneine.

Bedanke dich für das Interview.

The sporty rap

1. Listen to the rap.

2. Write in the missing words.

The sporty rap

I do it. It's ________ .

I like it when I ________ .

I do it. It's ________ .

I like it when I ________ .

I do it. It's ________ .

I like it when I ________ .

Playing, running, skating, riding after ________?

Yes, we ________ it!

Yes, we ________ it!

Yes, we ________ !

skate	fun	okay	run	great	play
	school	do	love	like	

3. Read the skipping rhymes.

Apples, peaches, pears and plums,
tell me when your birthday comes.
January, February, March …

I like coffee, I like tea,
I like Sally to jump with me.
One, two, three …

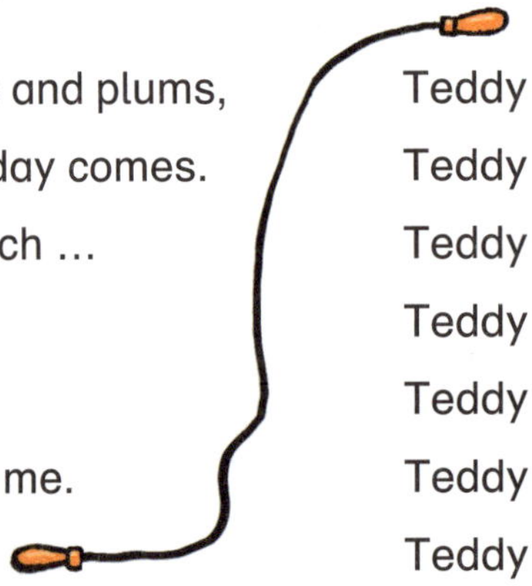

Teddy bear, teddy bear, turn around.
Teddy bear, teddy bear, touch the ground.
Teddy bear, teddy bear, show your shoe.
Teddy bear, teddy bear, that will do!
Teddy bear, teddy bear, go upstairs.
Teddy bear, teddy bear, say your prayers.
Teddy bear, teddy bear, turn out the light.
Teddy bear, teddy bear, say good night!

In the supermarket

1. Complete Sally's shopping list. Draw lines.

Sally's shopping list:

bread
eggs
milk
cheese
spinach
ice cream
biscuits
chocolate bars
lemonade
lollipops

2. Listen and tick ✓.

Phil's shopping list:

____

____

____

____

____

____

____

____

____

3. Write Phil's shopping list.

At the shopping centre

1. Listen and tick ✔ the correct answer.

The girls
want a CD by the Supergirls. ☐
the Fantastic Girls. ☐
the Superboys. ☐

Eric and Phil
go to the supermarket. ☐
the toy shop. ☐
the book shop. ☐

Liz
needs a new jacket. ☐
a T-shirt. ☐
socks. ☐

The girls
go to the cinema. ☐
the book shop. ☐
the sports shop. ☐

2. Listen. Cut out the speech bubbles (page 45), match and stick them in.

In the shop

Make up the dialogue. Write it down.

Frage, ob du dem Kunden helfen kannst.

Sage, was du kaufen möchtest.

Zeige dem Kunden die Ware.
Biete ihm an, sie anzuprobieren.

Bedanke dich.

Sage, dass dir das Kleidungsstück passt/gefällt. Frage, wie viel es kostet.

Nenne den Preis.

Bezahle.

Bedanke dich und verabschiede dich.

Verabschiede dich.

Jack and the beanstalk

1. Listen to the story.

2. Cut out the pictures (page 47), match and stick them in.

3. Cut out the speech bubbles (page 47), match and stick them in.

4. What fairy tales do you know? Show your books in class.

Detective Brighthead

1. Find the words.

traintaxistationcarferrybusunderground

2. Listen and draw Detective Brighthead's way.

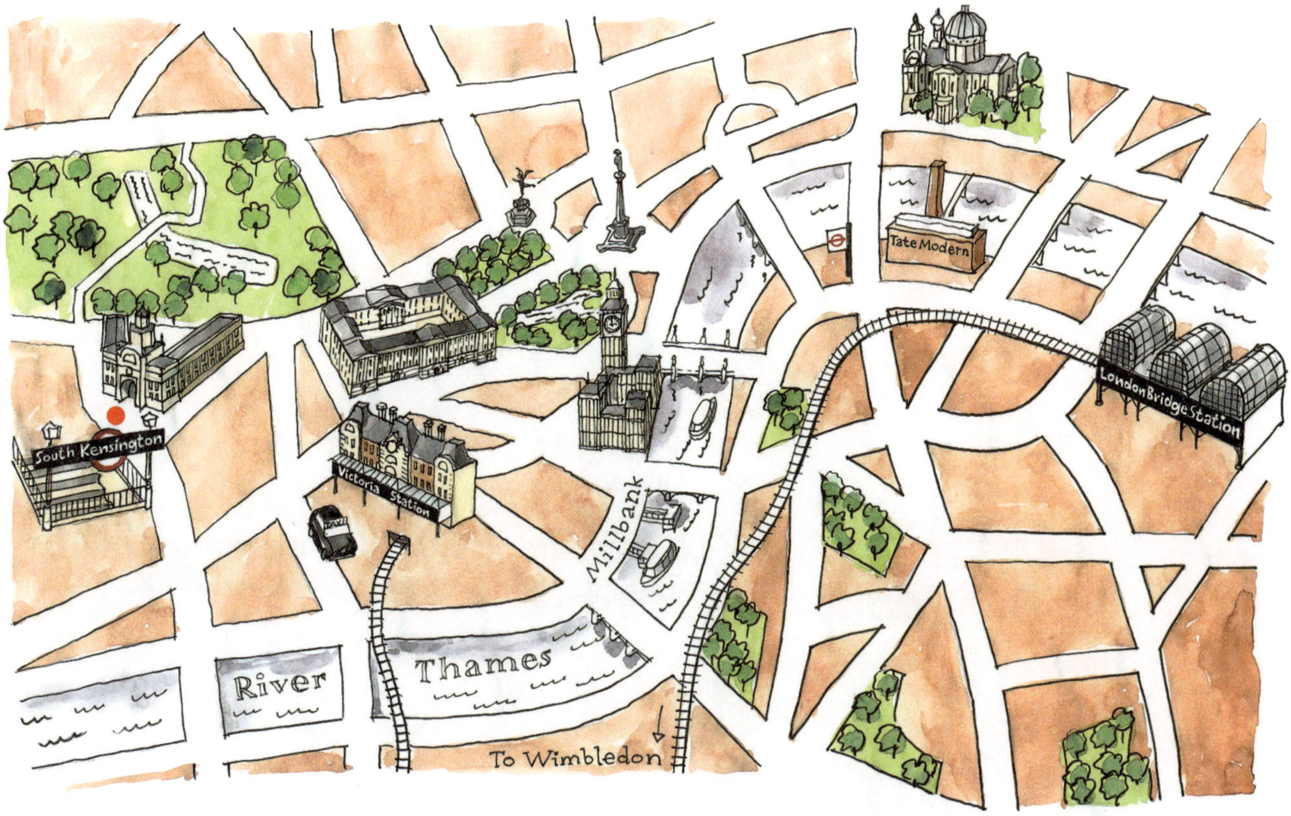

3. Complete the words.

__ __ain to London

b__ __ to London Bridge

__ __derground day card £5

The ticket is for the ________

The ticket is for the ________

The ticket is for the ________

Follow Detective Brighthead's way

Read the story and find the right way.
Circle ◯ the correct answers.
Your book can help you.

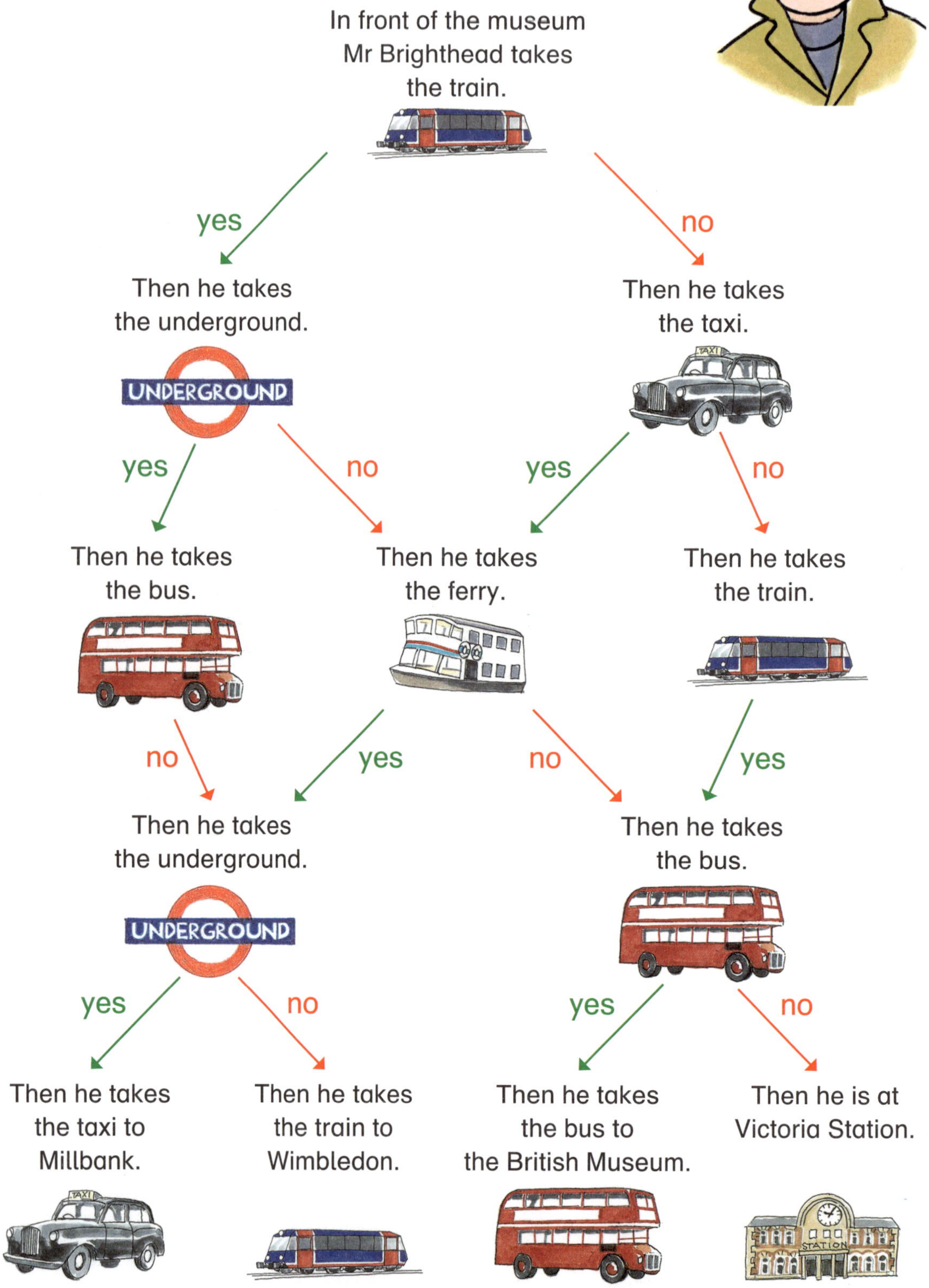

CLOCKMAKER 20 QUEEN'S ROAD

On the way

1. Listen and follow the grey route.

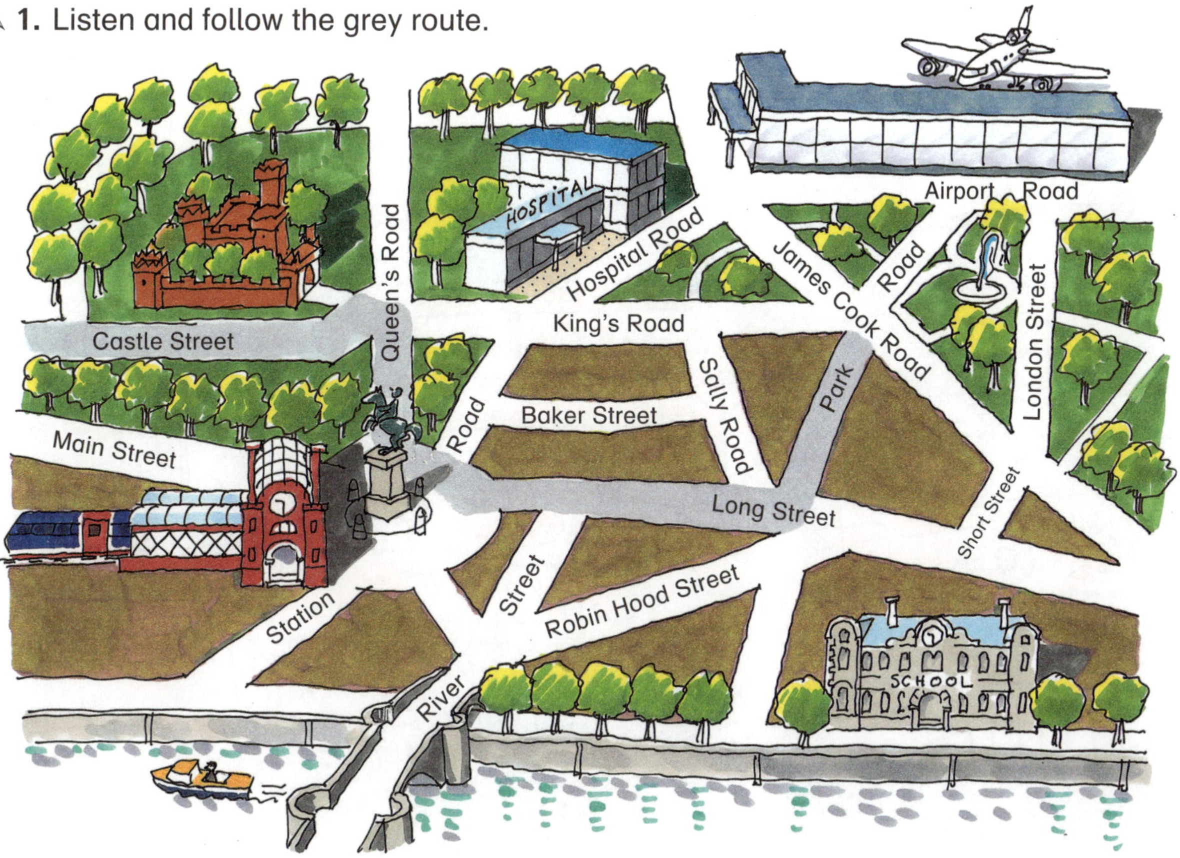

You arrive in ____________________ .

2. Listen and find your way.

route 1: You arrive _________________________.

route 2: You arrive _________________________.

3. Listen and draw lines.

Fasten your seat belts, please!

No smoking!

Put your seats in an upright position!

Switch off your mobile phones, radios and laptops!

Vehicles

Look at the picture and complete the sentences.

 Susan is going by ______________________ .

 Phil is going by ______________________ .

 Mr Brighthead ______________________ .

 Liz ______________________ .

 Eric ______________________ .

 Tim ______________________ .

 Emily ______________________ .

plane	ferry	car	bus	underground	train	taxi

Animals of the wild

1. Read and draw lines.

monkey	strong
elephant	clever
tortoise	big
lion	funny

2. Find the words.

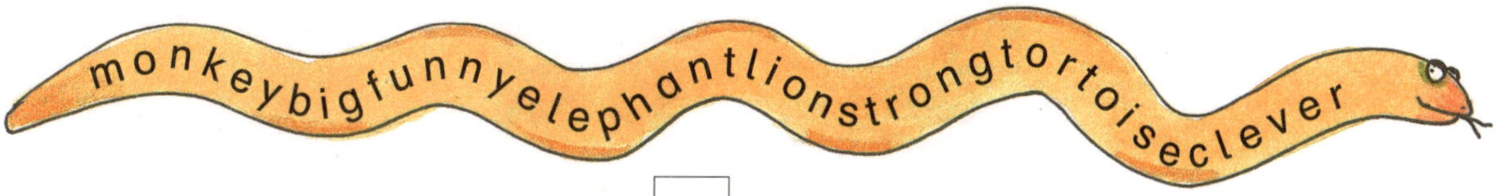

3. How many animals can you find? ☐
Write them down.

4. Do the crossword.

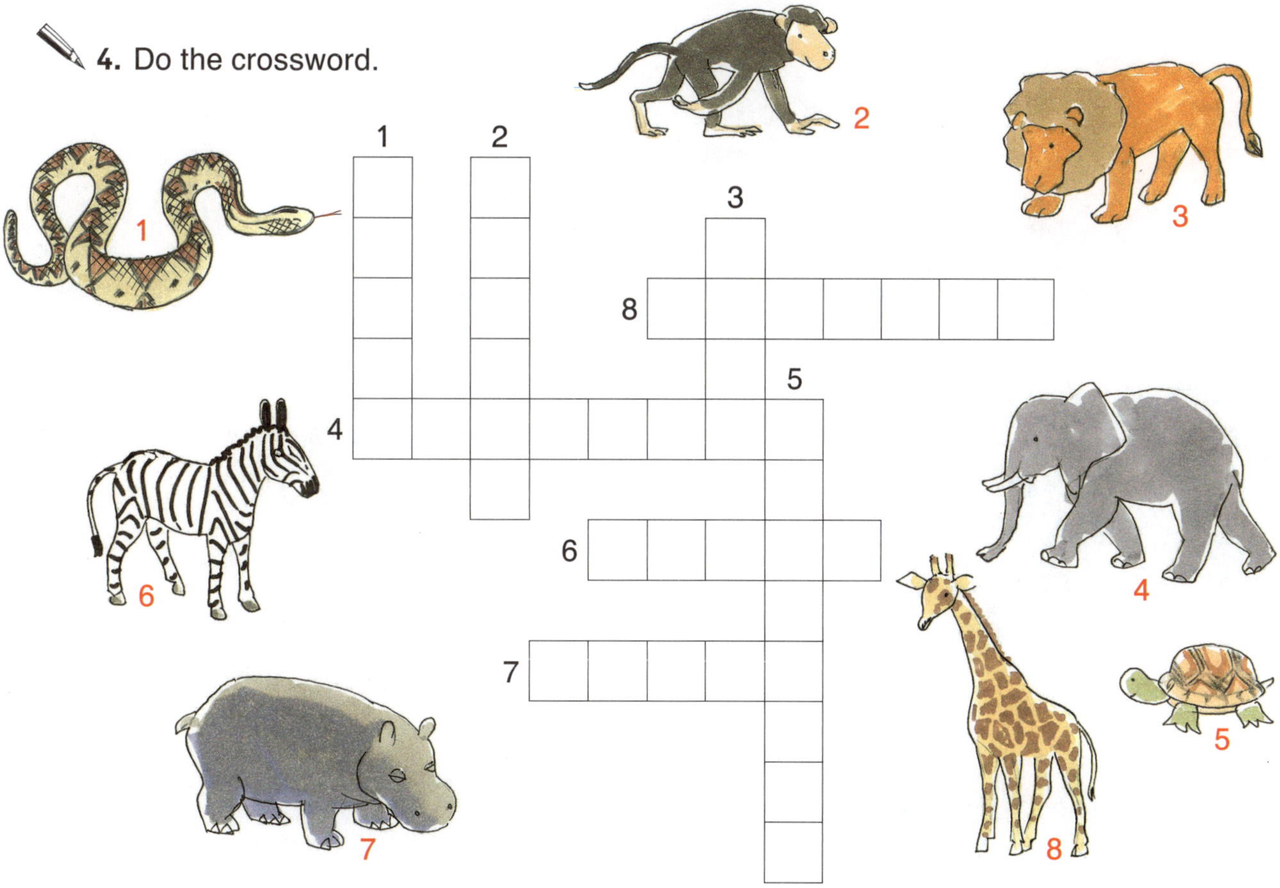

snake	giraffe	lion	zebra	monkey	elephant	hippo	tortoise

Detective Brighthead's trip to the jungle

1. Crazy photos! Which animal is it?
Number and write.

Wild animals

snake ☐ | tortoise ☐ | lion ☐ | zebra ☐

hippo ☐ | giraffe ☐ | monkey ☐ | elephant ☐

2. Crazy animals! What's wrong?

The ____________ is too ____________ .

The ____________ is too ____________ .

The ____________ is too ____________ .

The ____________ is too ____________ .

The ____________ is too ____________ .

fat	clever	strong	small	fast

3. Write word cards for an animal bingo.

Walking through the jungle

1. Listen to the song. Write in the missing words.

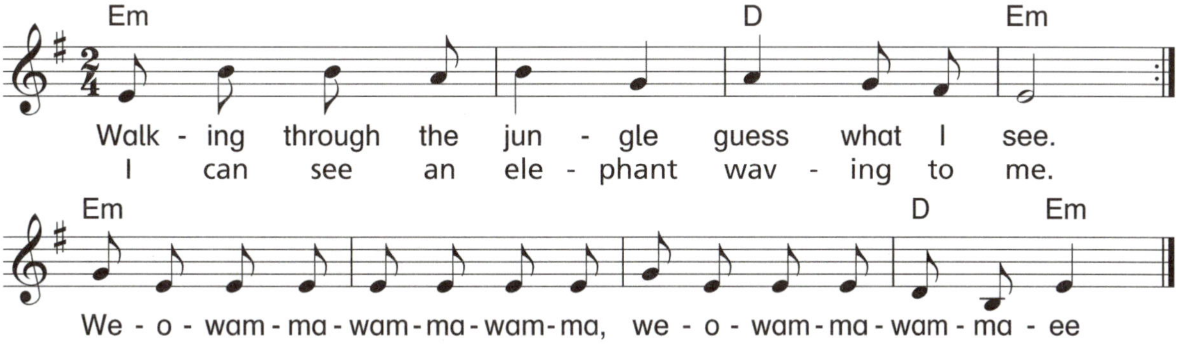

1. Walking through the  ______________________ , guess what I see?

   I can see an  ______________________ waving to me.

2. I can see a tall  ______________________ looking down at me.

3. I can see a  ______________________ swimming in the sea.

4. I can see a  ______________________ running fast to me.

5. I can see a  ______________________ climbing in a tree.

Can you go on? I can see ____

____ .

The clever tortoise

2. Listen and tick ✔: yes or no?

The tortoise, the monkey and the snake live in Africa.	yes	☐	no	☐
One day there is a big party.	yes	☐	no	☐
The zebra is the king of the jungle.	yes	☐	no	☐
The clever tortoise has got an idea.	yes	☐	no	☐
The hippo and the elephant play tennis.	yes	☐	no	☐
The tortoise plays a trick on the elephant and the hippo.	yes	☐	no	☐

At the doctor's

1. Number and write the words.

1 headache
2 neckache
3 earache
4 backache

2. Complete the speech bubbles.

I'm sick.

My ________ hurts.

I've got an ______________ .

I'm sick.

My ________ ________ .

I've got a ______________ .

I'm ________ .

My ________ ________ .

I've got a ______________ .

____

____

____

____

neck	ear	back	head	headache
backache	earache	neckache		

The inline skating accident

Listen. Cut out the speech bubbles (page 47), match and stick them in.

In Scotland

1. Where is Nessie? Write in: behind, under, in.

Nessie is

________ the boat.

Nessie is

________ Sally.

Nessie is

________ the lake.

2. Draw your own Nessie monster. Show your picture to your group.

3. Write the correct words under the pictures.

○ ____________________

○ ____________________

○ ____________________

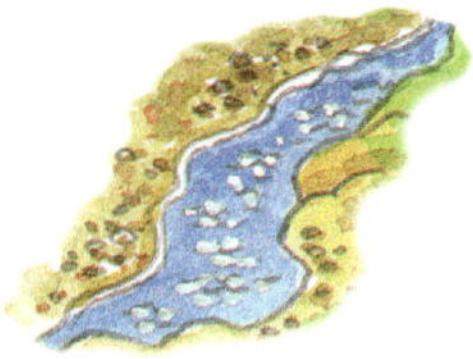

○ ____________________

○ ____________________

○ ____________________

river	mountain	lake	sea	Highland Games	castle

1 on Monday 2 on Tuesday 3 on Wednesday 4 on Thursday 5 on Friday

4. Listen, match the days of the week and number.

A trip to Scotland

1. Listen and number the Browns' route.

2. Find Nessie on the map. Nessie is ______________________________ .

3. Draw a tartan pattern.
Show it to your group.

Eric's jobs

1. Complete the sentences.

Monday

I __________________________ .

Tuesday

I __________________________ .

Wednesday

I __________________________ .

Thursday

I __________________________ .

Friday

I __________________________ .

Saturday

I __________________________ .

Sunday

I __________________________ .

make my bed	tidy my room	feed the cat	walk the dog
help in the kitchen	do my homework	help in the garden	

2. Listen, match the days of the week and draw lines. Which day is left over?

My cat likes to hide in boxes

1. Where are these cats from? Draw lines and write.

Germany
Greece
Japan
France
Spain

2. Complete the sentences.

Cat number 1 is from ____________________ .

Cat number 2 is ____________________ .

Cat number 3 ____________________ .

Cat number 4 ____________________ .

Cat number 5 ____________________ .

3. And this is my cat:

England
Italy
Poland
Turkey
Russia
USA
...

My cat is from ____________________ .

4. Show your picture to your group.

Looking for a penfriend

1. Fill in.

This is me: name: ______________________

boy/girl country: ______________________

age: __________

hobby: ______________________

I'm looking for: boy/girl country: ______________________

age: __________

2. And what are you looking for? Read your text to your class.

This is me: name: ______________________

boy/girl country: ______________________

age: __________

I'm looking for: boy/girl country: ______________________

age: __________

My hobbies are ____

____.

I can speak ____.

Let's be thankful!

1. Listen, colour and speak.
The apples are …

red, pink, blue, black,
green, orange, grey,
yellow, white, brown

2. Draw lines.

apples oranges cherries lemons

plums

pears

tomatoes corn

potatoes carrots beans

Corn on the cob

Prepare the cob.
Boil it for 5 to 10 minutes.
Serve it with butter and salt.
Enjoy your meal!

3. What are you thankful for? Write it down.

I'm thankful for

____

4. What happens on Carol's Thanksgiving Day? Read and draw lines.

In the evening	we go to the Thanksgiving parade.
In the morning	we watch the football match on TV.
In the afternoon	my mum puts the turkey into the oven.

A story about the first Thanksgiving

Little Bear | sees | a ship.

Little Bear | sees | some white people.

The Indians help | the white people | to build their houses, | to plant corn,

to hunt turkeys | and to catch fish.

The Indians | and the white people | have a big party:

the first Thanksgiving.

1. Write the story in your own Indian signs.
   Show it to your group.

2. Find out and learn about the American Indians in the internet.

Numbers (page 4)

Susan's room (page 11)

Through the day (page 16)

At eight o'clock in the morning I get up and eat. I have some milk and some cornflakes with sugar – so it's sweet.	At three o'clock in the afternoon school is over – hooray! I go home and watch TV, have fun with my friends and play.
At nine o'clock in the morning I'm already at school. I learn till I hear the bell ring for lunchtime and that's cool.	At eight o'clock in the evening I read and go to bed. Then I turn all the lights off and say: "Good night!" to Mum and Dad.

One day in the life of Alpha 72 (page 17)

At the shopping centre (page 24)

It's too big.

It's £25.

It's perfect. How much is it?

Yes, please. I'd like a new jacket.

Thank you.

Here are the jackets. Try them on.

Thank you. Goodbye.

Hello. Can I help you?

Here you are.

Schneidebogen

Jack and the beanstalk (page 26)

Here are five magic beans for your cow.

We must sell the cow.

I must climb it.

Now we can buy a new cow!

A castle, a kitchen and an apple pie. Yummy!

The inline skating accident (page 35)

What's the matter?

Ready, steady, go!

Let's go to the doctor's.

Next, please.

Your leg is broken.

My leg hurts so much. And my hand hurts, too.

Your hand is not broken. Put some ice on it.